Splinters

Splinters

Poems by

Charles K. Carter

© 2021 Charles K. Carter. All rights reserved.
This material may not be reproduced in any form, published,
reprinted, recorded, performed, broadcast,
rewritten or redistributed without
the explicit permission of Charles K. Carter.
All such actions are strictly prohibited by law.

Cover design by Shay Culligan

ISBN: 978-1-954353-16-9

Kelsay Books
502 South 1040 East, A-119
American Fork, Utah, 84003

For Babycakes

Acknowledgments

Thank you to these journals who initially published versions of the following pieces:

Anti-Heroin Chic: "The Bones of a Dancer"
Active Muse: "Mother"
Dodging the Rain: "Father," "Tribe," "When I Dream of the Ocean"
Idle Ink: "Sister"
Ink Pantry: "Garden of the Gods," "Irene," "Splinters"
Marias at Sampaguitas: "Wind"
The Mark Literary Review: "Earth"
Nymphs: "Fire"
The Raven Review: "Wolf"

Lazy Adventurer Publishing first published "The Moon" in the author's chapbook *Chasing Sunshine*.

Special thanks to David Blair, Brandon Carter, Andrea England, Christa Galvin, Eve Jones, and Christina Rice for their feedback and encouragement.

Contents

Mother	11
Earth	12
Tree Spirits	13
Wolf	14
eggs	15
Tick	16
Mining	17
Wind	18
Sister	19
Father	20
The Moon	21
The Bones of a Dancer	22
Garden of the Gods	23
Waging Wars	24
When I Knew You Loved Me	25
Weather	26
Blue Eyes	27
Whisky	28
Vampire	29
Irene	30
Tribe	31
Fire	32
Snowmen Lovers	33
Roller Rink	34
Searching	35
Blue	36
When I Dream of the Ocean	37
Glue	38
Bottom Feeder	39
Water	40
Splinters	41

Mother

The circles under her eyes are dark, hair is shiny, shoulders
    slouched.
The soles of her shoes are as worn as her weathered face,
taking my tiny fingers in hand, she gently leads me across the
    desert.

Tired from walking, she has a spirit that flies higher than the
    vultures.
She finds a way to smile through the burning, blinding sun,
to smile through scalding sands and dirty water that remains in the
    canteen.

The gods created her with the strength of the canyons, holding up
    the sky.
The gods created her with a capacity to love greater than all water
    the oceans can hold,
greater than all the rain the clouds can cry.
                        This is mother. This is Mother.

Earth

The creature walks barefoot on this earth,
feeling a connection to the dirt,
stepping softly, leaving pawprints that fade away with the rain.
The creature takes just what it needs from the earth and nothing
    more.
When her time comes,
she lies down and dies, leaving her body exposed,
unafraid to be devoured by the vultures
because she knows that her spirit will then fly.

Man walks with feet covered in waterproof boots,
forging a barrier between himself and the earth,
afraid to get dirty.
He stamps through the jungle,
flora and fauna falling at his feet,
bringing down whole ecosystems as he exists.
He makes his harsh mark on this world.
He takes more than what he needs, devours all that he can
because if he is distracted by excess:
fast cars, iPhones, the finest of fashion,
he will not have to face his own wrongdoings.
When man's time comes,
he is buried in the earth,
hiding his Spirit-House,
preventing his spirit from flying free.

Tree Spirits

Humans like to think they are
the highest form of being
in their fleshy wrappers, meat
centers, and their unquenched taste
for destruction. In their few
decades, they stir no magic,
only chaos.

Trees are the highest form of
rebirth. To be reborn a
tree is to be strong, giving,
resistant to change—to sit
and observe the world's beauty
for hundreds of years in great
peace, in stillness.

Wolf

Imagine the natural
pull of the wolf to the
moon, a pull so deep, the
wolf cannot contain it-
self but must howl to let
the whole world know that though
he does not know why, he
is in love with that moon.

I am that wolf and you
are that moon. I, a trapped
beast in my cave, weeping
the spring high tide and the
unwitting loss of a
new moon.

eggs

when daddy left
all the eggs I cracked had blood spots
mamma said to scoop out the spot
and keep the rest

when mamma left too
all the eggs I cracked had maggots
I decided it best to throw out
whole cartons

when he decides to leave
when he decides he don't love me
there will be no shells to step on
there's no eggs in my house

no more

Tick

What happens to a tick if
you don't remove it? Does it
swell up and explode on your
sweet juices like your lover
who met you in the woods where
this tick first took hold? Or does
it burrow way into your
skin, living to fill the space
that he has left inside you?

Mining

We keep mining the
earth for what is actually
found in our own hearts.

Wind

Heed the power and the warning of the mother winds.

She has looked upon man and carried the seductive songs of sirens
    to their ears,
false hope for the longing-to-be-touched, lonely traveler.

She has curated twisters across the Midwest, hurricanes in the
    tropics,
carrying lucky pennies, Chihuahuas, and lost hope across this
    earth.

She has blown out their light, leaving them in great darkness,
forcing them to face their fears, their regrets, their inner demons.

Men run for safety not knowing that she has power
to blow them out of existence in mere seconds, snuffing their
    inner-light.

Heed the power and the warning of the mother winds.
        She sees all: she knows our history and won't let us
        repeat it again.

Sister

Sister, they always said we were the bright ones, the ones who were going to go so far, but here we are, only twenty-five miles from the house that wasn't a home, twenty-five miles from the man who's staticky voice taught us that we were much less worthy than what we ever were.

Sister, they always said we were the pretty ones, the ones whose smiles were transmittable, but the only thing that seems to transmit to us is our need to not be alone at night, the need to tear ourselves down so we can fall into someone, anyone's jagged arms.

Sister, they always said we could make it, if we put our minds to it, we could do anything, we could be anyone, but twenty-five miles isn't far enough from that radio signal of hate, that frequency of terror. We smile but underneath it, we are barely there.

Father

There was a crow's nest outside my window.
I would watch the father crow guard his little one
while the mother went out for food.

There was a crow's nest outside my window.
I would watch the father crow teach the little one
to squawk and flap his downy wings.

There was a crow's nest outside my window.
I stepped out on the branch over abandoned nest,
I spread my arms and tried to fly.

There was a crow's nest outside my window.
I wanted to be his child, his little hatchling.
I wanted to make someone proud.

The Moon

My eyes fell down in shame, avoiding your nakedness, lit only by
    the moon.
Sand between our toes, rushing to the water's cool cover, lit only
    by the moon.

My eyes filled with laughter, sunsets, silhouettes, and lighthouses,
    trampoline jumping,
making paychecks rain, falling quickly, a teenager hypnotized by
    the light of the moon.

My eyes filled with wonder, dancing in your simple touch, hands
    intertwined,
legs locked underwater, softly kissing, teasing hands, skin white as
    the summer moon.

My eyes clenched shut, wings pinned by the weight of your elbows
    against my bare back,
biting pillows, first in a long line of victims whose muffled cries
    were heard only by the moon.

The Bones of a Dancer

The bones of a dancer
do not simply fade away like the final note
in a grand opera or a beautiful ballet
The bones of a dancer
do not give up as the valediction
written on a page
from one lover to another
Words forced too hard
for too long
Words
lose their meanings

The bones of a dancer
do not give up the fight
like a battered child
or an abused mother
Dancers dance anyway
far too long
Past
their supposed prime

From learner to teacher
from dancer to dancer
their bones do not fade
but crash violently
to an
end
like that of a black hole
giving birth to something greater
once again

The bones of a dancer know
a bone once broken
heals stronger

Garden of the Gods

I stand upon this rock where we had our second date,
then both spent and energized from lovemaking,
dazed by the camel-shaped formation, the gods' fate

that brought us here, miles from any sound but these beating
    hearts,
longing to be lost in each other's touch again,
we climbed higher, fell deeper, believing we would never part

but as the space between the camel's hump and its head grows,
so does the space between us now, both physical and beyond,
this space, this emptiness, this forest full of woes.

Every year someone falls to their death—
dazed by the dizzying distance below, I find my footing,
pondering what hope for us there is left.

Waging Wars

As winter's wars wage on
between the plow and the road,
between the sickness and the cure,
between the river and the skates—
the moon-white snow drifts at the end of the driveway,
building just as our next fight builds.

When I Knew You Loved Me

When I knew you loved me,
when I knew it was real,
I was reminded of
Newton's third law about
opposite reactions.
I hid myself in my
bedroom, curled up in a
ball in corner, behind
my grandmother's arm
chair, and cried and cried and
cried. When you found me, you
asked me what was wrong. I
answered, *If our love is
this good, then something bad
will have to happen. It's
only science, my love.*

Weather

Anger is the clouds
rolling through my morning tea.
I keep on sipping.

Blue Eyes

She got blue eyes that
pierce like the red sun spilling
over a black mount.

She got a fire that
could melt all the cold hearts in
this cross, bitter world.

She got a fierceness
like daggers cutting through the
flesh of the unjust.

She got a will to
carry on after the world
she loved is all gone.

All I got from her
is her blue eyes. Why not her
will? Why not her fire?

Whisky

Broken hearts are the
fire in a shot of whisky:
calming over time.

Vampire

Her mother was not
stable. She went with the first
man to invite her

inside. He kept her
down with his words and with his
fists. She would wake up

to him drawing lines
on her naked back with his
pocketknife. He fed

off her blood. He thought
he was making her weaker.
Unknowingly, he

carved her wings to fly.

Irene

Irene took quickly to the scene,
looking to discover new things,
looking to be places she'd never been.

Irene quickly became a yes woman all right,
saying yes to the men's aberrant advances
and yes to the women's aimless advice.

Irene took quickly to saying yes
becoming addicted to their requests,
a few more track marks on her arms,

a few more heads up her skirt.
Irene quickly became a no woman all right.
She became no woman all right.

Tribe

The lion hunts those who fall from the herd.
Tribe does the same, carefully picks its prey.
She's a witch. An adulterer. Slut. Whore.
He's a communist. Fag. A terrorist.
Fear immigrants. Natives. The different.
Feed them to the lions. Grab your pitchfork.
Tie her to the stake. Light her up in flames.
No more screams. Not a single peep or sound.
Watch Lady Liberty burn to the ground.

Fire

Fire is in man's hands.
He can use it as a tool.
The warmth of a fireplace. Lighting of a gas grill. Warding off
    disease.
But man is not responsible for his gift. For he is selfish.
He uses his tools not just for good. But for evil.
He torches the towers of those he does not understand.
He burns the flesh of those who do not agree with him.
Lit tires stuck burning the flesh of his enemy's meaty midsections
upwards and outwards.
Until all that is left
are ruins.

Fire is in Mother Nature's almighty hands.
She holds the true power.
To ignite with lightning. To burn through the evil forests that are
    man.
To burn their houses and their white picket fences.
To burn their history: their holy books and photographs.
She has the power to destroy
but with her great love,
new life forms.
A dandelion rises
from the ash.

Snowmen Lovers

Crystals grew from the trees and created
iridescent chandeliers for snowmen
lovers to dance under, knowing that once
the sun peaked high in the sky again, that
their smiles would melt away.

Roller Rink

*NSYNC and Shania Twain are all the
old couple who owns the roller rink knows
how to play but we sing and dance and skate
anyway. Couples clumsily dance and
fall into each other's arms, hands to hold
each other steady. The roller rink is
where one can show their teenage heart to the
world. He grabbed my ~~heart~~ hand and then set me free,
spinning to the wall, bracing my broken
heart for the limbo; exiting the rink
for candy at the concessions when the
couple's skate to "From this Moment On" starts.

Searching

The water drips off
the kayak's white oar, searching
for its way back home.

Blue

when I meditate
I find myself floating
light feather down

a clear creek lined with
smooth river rock flying by
a fruitful green tree

over a red clay
bluff and into the deep
blue sea—all around

me is nothing but
blue refracting rays of light
from the world above

the blue silence
a womb in its comfort and
its serenity

it's always quiet
at first stuck in the blue but
then comes the eye of

god with her whalesong
guardian of deep keeping
me in light—in peace.

When I Dream of the Ocean

When I dream of the ocean, I dream of your face.
I dream of the scent of sunscreen, sensual hands on back,
closed eyes, kissed by the shine of another sunny day.

When I dream of the ocean, I dream of the smooth caramel sand
spackled on the back of your bright white legs,
freckled like fresh strawberry lemonade like the back of your
        hands.

When I dream of the ocean, I dream of the high tide
that washed away the sand from our feet
and the gleam from your chocolate pudding eyes.

When I dream of the ocean, I dream of tropical storms,
of tidal waves and riptides and hurricanes
taking away all that is good and sunny and warm.

When I dream of the ocean, I dream of your broken sandals found
        in the estuary.
I thought you were lost to the sea until I saw you in that
        Midwestern café.
You were not lost to the sea, only lost by choice, lost lost to me.

Glue

I used to think you
were the glue that held this broken heart together

but baby now that
all the floodwater has receded, I see it

was me who held it
together all along. It
was me. It was me.

Bottom Feeder

There is a myth that in the Amazon,
the river dolphins sprout legs, come ashore,
and, in disguise, they dance the night away.

I have a theory that you were
a bottom feeder birthed in the
murky Mississippi waters.
You came ashore disguised as a
former lover—wide eyes, thick lips,
lashes instead of whiskers,
lashes wisping against my cheek
as you fed on the salt of my
skin, sucking the life force from my
soul. I thought I could have loved you.

Morning came. You returned to the river,
returned to the deep but one of these days,
I will hook you. You will return to me.

Water

A celestial cry from somewhere deep in the cosmos calls me to the
        sea
I make pilgrimage back to the waters of my ancient ancestors

The rippled ringlets distort my reflection on the water's edge
The knife cuts the skin and my legs split the water's clear surface

My blood flows from me like a soprano's soothing swan song
The red dissipates, swallowed by the surrounding blue

I hear the call from the cosmos, gentle whalesong
Guiding me home, bringing peaceful clarity.

Splinters

I have found solace in this fluid state, this comforting womb,
this escape from the reality of mankind's mania,
drawn to the water's stillness, its silence, to its blue

but the waves have torn off this false merman tale
and spat me out saltily to the sands above
bidding me no mercy, no protection as the ancient whale

waves a gentle goodbye—I bring my wet, wrinkled fingertips
to brush away these ocean-like teardrops.
I pluck away the barnacles like scabs that have to be compulsively
    picked

off like a fish being scaled, flaked until it is merely flesh to be
    devoured.
I am no longer welcome to live in a world where there is only
    peace.
I stand vulnerable: human, naked, exposed, scoured.

I step out of the water and find footing on solid ground,
gravity weighing heavy on these shoulders
taking in the sights of the green earth and the sky's musical sounds

channeling the mighty thunder of the gods to stand tall, to stay
    afloat.
Even though I fear the wind will whisk me away to mere particles
    of dust
as the hurricane makes splinters of a small, wooden fishing boat.

I would rather be splintered in the sea.

About the Author

Charles K. Carter is a queer poet and educator from Iowa. He shares his home with his artist husband and his spoiled pets. He enjoys film, yoga, and live music. Melissa Etheridge is his ultimate obsession. He holds an MFA in writing from Lindenwood University. His poems have appeared in several literary journals. He is the author of *Chasing Sunshine* (Lazy Adventurer Publishing). Carter has two forthcoming collections of poetry: *Salem Revisited* (WordTech Editions) and *Read My Lips* (David Robert Books).

Connect on Twitter, Facebook, and Instagram @CKCpoetry

www.CKCpoetry.com

www.ingramcontent.com/pod-product-compliance
Lightning Source LLC
Chambersburg PA
CBHW071641090426
42738CB00013B/3182